CLARINET

2ND EDITION

THE BEST OF
The Beatles

ISBN 978-0-7935-2143-2

HAL•LEONARD®
CORPORATION
7777 W. BLUEMOUND RD. P.O. BOX 13819 MILWAUKEE, WI 53213

Visit Hal Leonard Online at
www.halleonard.com

CONTENTS

ALL MY LOVING

CLARINET

Words and Music by JOHN LENNON
and PAUL McCARTNEY

ACROSS THE UNIVERSE

Clarinet

Words and Music by JOHN LENNON
and PAUL McCARTNEY

Slowly and smoothly

ALL YOU NEED IS LOVE

Clarinet

Words and Music by JOHN LENNON
and PAUL McCARTNEY

AND I LOVE HER

CLARINET

Words and Music by JOHN LENNON and PAUL McCARTNEY

Gently

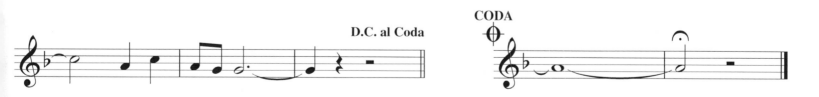

BACK IN THE U.S.S.R.

Clarinet

Words and Music by JOHN LENNON
and PAUL McCARTNEY

THE BALLAD OF JOHN AND YOKO

Clarinet

Words and Music by JOHN LENNON
and PAUL McCARTNEY

BECAUSE

CLARINET

Words and Music by JOHN LENNON
and PAUL McCARTNEY

BIRTHDAY

CLARINET

Words and Music by JOHN LENNON
and PAUL McCARTNEY

Moderately fast Rock

BLACKBIRD

CLARINET

Words and Music by JOHN LENNON
and PAUL McCARTNEY

CAN'T BUY ME LOVE

Clarinet

Words and Music by JOHN LENNON
and PAUL McCARTNEY

COME TOGETHER

CLARINET

Words and Music by JOHN LENNON
and PAUL McCARTNEY

Slowly

A DAY IN THE LIFE

Clarinet

Words and Music by JOHN LENNON
and PAUL McCARTNEY

DAY TRIPPER

Clarinet

Words and Music by JOHN LENNON
and PAUL McCARTNEY

DEAR PRUDENCE

CLARINET

Words and Music by JOHN LENNON
and PAUL McCARTNEY

DO YOU WANT TO KNOW A SECRET?

CLARINET

Words and Music by JOHN LENNON
and PAUL McCARTNEY

DRIVE MY CAR

CLARINET

Words and Music by JOHN LENNON
and PAUL McCARTNEY

Moderately, with a beat

EIGHT DAYS A WEEK

Clarinet

Words and Music by JOHN LENNON
and PAUL McCARTNEY

ELEANOR RIGBY

CLARINET

Words and Music by JOHN LENNON
and PAUL McCARTNEY

EVERY LITTLE THING

Clarinet

Words and Music by JOHN LENNON
and PAUL McCARTNEY

THE FOOL ON THE HILL

Clarinet

Words and Music by JOHN LENNON
and PAUL McCARTNEY

FROM ME TO YOU

Clarinet

Words and Music by JOHN LENNON
and PAUL McCARTNEY

GET BACK

CLARINET

Words and Music by JOHN LENNON
and PAUL McCARTNEY

GIRL

CLARINET

Words and Music by JOHN LENNON
and PAUL McCARTNEY

GOLDEN SLUMBERS

CLARINET

Words and Music by JOHN LENNON
and PAUL McCARTNEY

Moderately

GOOD DAY SUNSHINE

Clarinet

Words and Music by JOHN LENNON
and PAUL McCARTNEY

GOT TO GET YOU INTO MY LIFE

Clarinet

Words and Music by JOHN LENNON
and PAUL McCARTNEY

A HARD DAY'S NIGHT

Clarinet

Words and Music by JOHN LENNON
and PAUL McCARTNEY

HELLO, GOODBYE

CLARINET

Words and Music by JOHN LENNON
and PAUL McCARTNEY

HELP!

CLARINET

Words and Music by JOHN LENNON
and PAUL McCARTNEY

HELTER SKELTER

CLARINET

Words and Music by JOHN LENNON
and PAUL McCARTNEY

HERE COMES THE SUN

CLARINET

Words and Music by
GEORGE HARRISON

HERE, THERE AND EVERYWHERE

Clarinet

Words and Music by JOHN LENNON
and PAUL McCARTNEY

HEY JUDE

CLARINET

Words and Music by JOHN LENNON
and PAUL McCARTNEY

I FEEL FINE

CLARINET

Words and Music by JOHN LENNON
and PAUL McCARTNEY

I AM THE WALRUS

Clarinet

Words and Music by JOHN LENNON
and PAUL McCARTNEY

Slowly

I SAW HER STANDING THERE

Clarinet

Words and Music by JOHN LENNON
and PAUL McCARTNEY

Moderately bright, with a beat

I SHOULD HAVE KNOWN BETTER

Clarinet

Words and Music by JOHN LENNON
and PAUL McCARTNEY

I WANT TO HOLD YOUR HAND

CLARINET

Words and Music by JOHN LENNON
and PAUL McCARTNEY

Moderately

I WILL

CLARINET

Words and Music by JOHN LENNON
and PAUL McCARTNEY

Moderately

I'LL CRY INSTEAD

CLARINET

Words and Music by JOHN LENNON
and PAUL McCARTNEY

I'LL FOLLOW THE SUN

CLARINET

Words and Music by JOHN LENNON
and PAUL McCARTNEY

I'M A LOSER

CLARINET

Words and Music by JOHN LENNON
and PAUL McCARTNEY

Moderately

I'M HAPPY JUST TO DANCE WITH YOU

CLARINET

Words and Music by JOHN LENNON
and PAUL McCARTNEY

48

I'VE JUST SEEN A FACE

CLARINET

Words and Music by JOHN LENNON
and PAUL McCARTNEY

IF I FELL

CLARINET

Words and Music by JOHN LENNON
and PAUL McCARTNEY

IN MY LIFE

CLARINET

Words and Music by JOHN LENNON
and PAUL McCARTNEY

IT WON'T BE LONG

Clarinet

Words and Music by JOHN LENNON
and PAUL McCARTNEY

IT'S ONLY LOVE

CLARINET

Words and Music by JOHN LENNON
and PAUL McCARTNEY

JULIA

Clarinet

Words and Music by JOHN LENNON
and PAUL McCARTNEY

LADY MADONNA

Clarinet

Words and Music by JOHN LENNON
and PAUL McCARTNEY

LET IT BE

Clarinet

Words and Music by JOHN LENNON
and PAUL McCARTNEY

THE LONG AND WINDING ROAD

CLARINET

Words and Music by JOHN LENNON
and PAUL McCARTNEY

LOVE ME DO

Clarinet

Words and Music by JOHN LENNON
and PAUL McCARTNEY

LUCY IN THE SKY WITH DIAMONDS

Clarinet

Words and Music by JOHN LENNON
and PAUL McCARTNEY

MAGICAL MYSTERY TOUR

CLARINET

Words and Music by JOHN LENNON
and PAUL McCARTNEY

MARTHA MY DEAR

Clarinet

Words and Music by JOHN LENNON
and PAUL McCARTNEY

MICHELLE

Clarinet

Words and Music by JOHN LENNON
and PAUL McCARTNEY

NO REPLY

CLARINET

Words and Music by JOHN LENNON
and PAUL McCARTNEY

NORWEGIAN WOOD

(This Bird Has Flown)

Clarinet

Words and Music by JOHN LENNON
and PAUL McCARTNEY

NOWHERE MAN

CLARINET

Words and Music by JOHN LENNON
and PAUL McCARTNEY

Moderately bright

OB-LA-DI, OB-LA-DA

Clarinet

Words and Music by JOHN LENNON
and PAUL McCARTNEY

OCTOPUS'S GARDEN

CLARINET

Words and Music by RICHARD STARKEY,
JOHN LENNON and PAUL McCARTNEY

PAPERBACK WRITER

Words and Music by JOHN LENNON
and PAUL McCARTNEY

Clarinet

Bright Rock

PENNY LANE

Clarinet

Words and Music by JOHN LENNON
and PAUL McCARTNEY

PLEASE PLEASE ME

Clarinet

Words and Music by JOHN LENNON
and PAUL McCARTNEY

P.S. I LOVE YOU

CLARINET

Words and Music by JOHN LENNON
and PAUL McCARTNEY

Moderate Rock

REVOLUTION

Clarinet

Words and Music by JOHN LENNON
and PAUL McCARTNEY

Moderate Rock and Roll Shuffle

72

RUN FOR YOUR LIFE

Clarinet

Words and Music by JOHN LENNON
and PAUL McCARTNEY

Copyright © 1965 Sony/ATV Music Publishing LLC
Copyright Renewed
All Rights Administered by Sony/ATV Music Publishing LLC, 8 Music Square West, Nashville, TN 37203
International Copyright Secured   All Rights Reserved

SGT. PEPPER'S LONELY HEARTS CLUB BAND

Clarinet

Words and Music by JOHN LENNON
and PAUL McCARTNEY

SHE LOVES YOU

Clarinet

Words and Music by JOHN LENNON
and PAUL McCARTNEY

SHE'S A WOMAN

Clarinet

Words and Music by JOHN LENNON
and PAUL McCARTNEY

SOMETHING

Clarinet

Words and Music by
GEORGE HARRISON

STRAWBERRY FIELDS FOREVER

Clarinet

Words and Music by JOHN LENNON
and PAUL McCARTNEY

TELL ME WHY

Clarinet

Words and Music by JOHN LENNON and PAUL McCARTNEY

THANK YOU GIRL

Clarinet

Words and Music by JOHN LENNON
and PAUL McCARTNEY

THINGS WE SAID TODAY

Clarinet

Words and Music by JOHN LENNON
and PAUL McCARTNEY

THIS BOY
(Ringo's Theme)

Clarinet

Words and Music by JOHN LENNON
and PAUL McCARTNEY

TICKET TO RIDE

Words and Music by JOHN LENNON
and PAUL McCARTNEY

Flute

Moderate Rock

TWIST AND SHOUT

Clarinet

Words and Music by BERT RUSSELL
and PHIL MEDLEY

WE CAN WORK IT OUT

Clarinet

Words and Music by JOHN LENNON
and PAUL McCARTNEY

WHEN I'M SIXTY-FOUR

Clarinet

Words and Music by JOHN LENNON
and PAUL McCARTNEY

WHILE MY GUITAR GENTLY WEEPS

CLARINET

Words and Music by
GEORGE HARRISON

WITH A LITTLE HELP FROM MY FRIENDS

Clarinet

Words and Music by JOHN LENNON
and PAUL McCARTNEY

THE WORD

CLARINET

Words and Music by JOHN LENNON
and PAUL McCARTNEY

YELLOW SUBMARINE

CLARINET

Words and Music by JOHN LENNON
and PAUL McCARTNEY

YES IT IS

CLARINET

Words and Music by JOHN LENNON
and PAUL McCARTNEY

YESTERDAY

CLARINET

Words and Music by JOHN LENNON
and PAUL McCARTNEY

Moderately

YOU CAN'T DO THAT

Clarinet

Words and Music by JOHN LENNON
and PAUL McCARTNEY

YOU WON'T SEE ME

Clarinet

Words and Music by JOHN LENNON
and PAUL McCARTNEY

YOU'RE GOING TO LOSE THAT GIRL

Clarinet

Words and Music by JOHN LENNON
and PAUL McCARTNEY

YOU'VE GOT TO HIDE YOUR LOVE AWAY

CLARINET

Words and Music by JOHN LENNON
and PAUL McCARTNEY

YOUR MOTHER SHOULD KNOW

CLARINET

Words and Music by JOHN LENNON
and PAUL McCARTNEY